CREEPY, KOOKY SCIENCE

Icky Insects

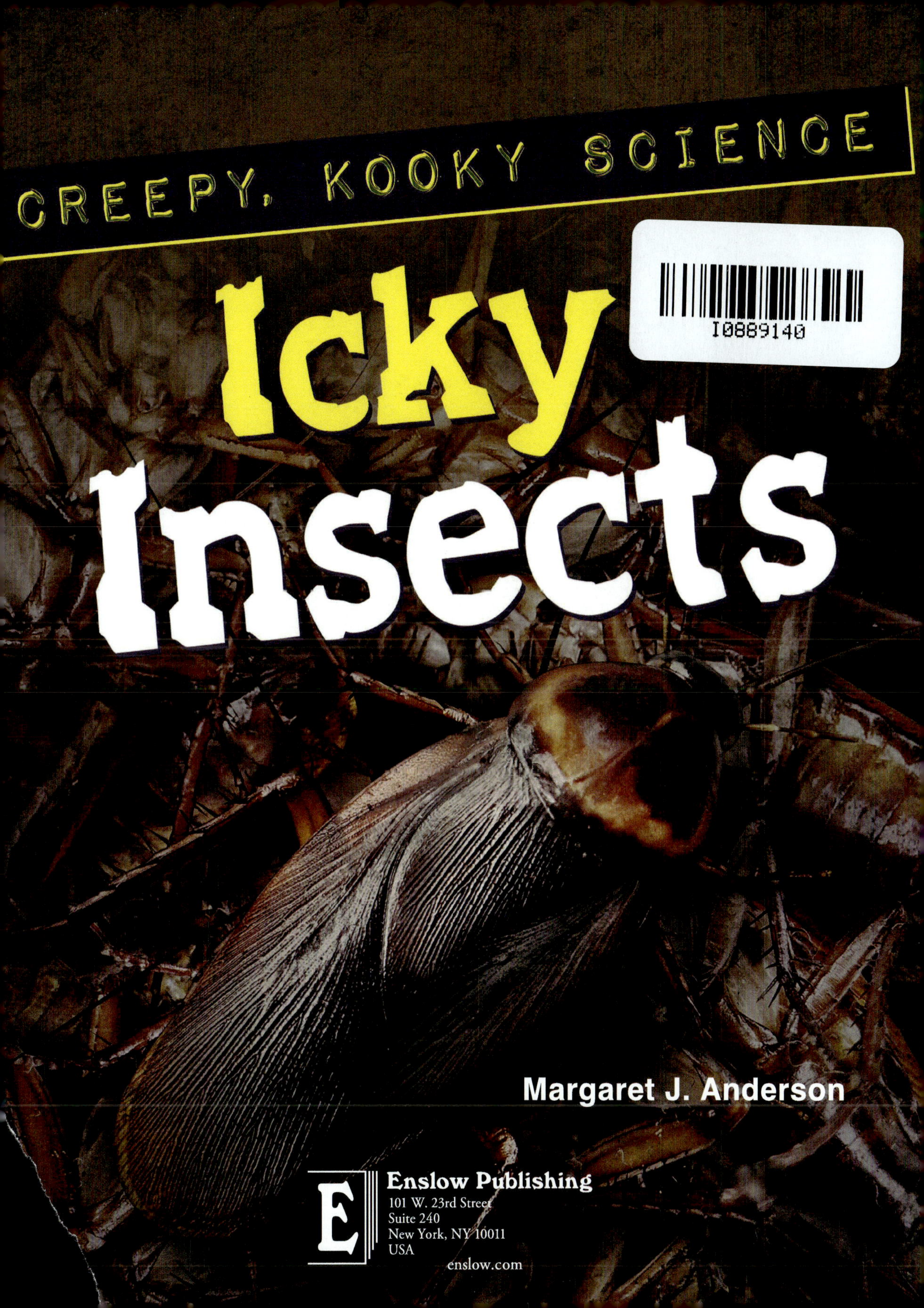

Margaret J. Anderson

Enslow Publishing
101 W. 23rd Street
Suite 240
New York, NY 10011
USA
enslow.com

Published in 2019 by Enslow Publishing, LLC.
101 W. 23rd Street, Suite 240, New York, NY 10011

Library of Congress Cataloging-in-Publication Data

Names: Anderson, Margaret J. author.
Title: Icky insects / Margaret J. Anderson.
Description: New York : Enslow Publishing, 2019. | Series: Creepy, kooky science | Audience: Grade 5-8. | Includes bibliographical references and index.
Identifiers: LCCN 2018012318| ISBN 9781978504493 (library bound) | ISBN 9781978505506 (paperback)
Subjects: LCSH: Insects—Juvenile literature.
Classification: LCC QL467.2 .A53 2019 | DDC 595.7—dc23
LC record available at https://lccn.loc.gov/2018012318

To Our Readers: We have done our best to make sure all websites in this book were active and appropriate when we went to press. However, the author and the publisher have no control over and assume no liability for the material available on those websites or on any websites they may link to. Any comments or suggestions can be sent by email to customerservice@enslow.com.

Portions of this book originally appeared in *Bugged-Out Insects*.

Photo Credits: Cover, p. 1 Dejawu/Shutterstock.com; p. 5 Mark Garlick/Science Photo Library/Getty Images; p. 8 tony mills/Shutterstock.com; p. 12 Kim Howell/Shutterstock.com; p. 14 Charoenkrung.Studio99/Shutterstock.com; p. 16 Vladimir Wrangel/Shutterstock.com; p. 18 Mrs. Sucharut Chounyoo/Shutterstock.com; p. 20 neil hardwick/Shutterstock.com; p. 22 Tacio Philip Sansonovski/Shutterstock.com; p. 25 Andrey Armyagov/Shutterstock .com; p. 27 Young Swee Ming/Shutterstock.com; p. 30 rtbilder/Shutterstock.com; p. 33 Pavel Krasensky/Shutterstock.com; p. 35 Susan Liebenberg/Shutterstock.com; p. 38 Simon Shim/Shutterstock.com; p. 40 Michael Potter11/Shutterstock.com.

Contents

Introduction

Long before the age of the dinosaur, cockroaches scuttled through the giant club mosses and ferns. Before pterodactyls took to the air, giant dragonflies with a 30-inch (76-centimeter) wingspan swooped over the swampy land. Insects have been around for more than three hundred million years. They will likely still be here when the rest of us are gone.

One reason insects are survivors is that they have a hard shell-like exoskeleton. They wear their skeletons on the outside. This is good protection. Creatures with an exoskeleton belong to a group called arthropods. Spiders, centipedes, and millipedes are also arthropods. You can tell if an arthropod is an insect by counting its legs. Insects have only six legs. As if to make up for having fewer legs than other arthropods, most insects have wings. When danger strikes, they can fly off to new places. Even with a hundred legs, you can't cover much ground when the going gets tough.

Three hundred million years ago, dragonflies as big as birds ruled the air.

Insects are found everywhere. They live indoors and outdoors. They live above ground and underground. They are found on snow-capped mountains and in tropical jungles. There are more than two hundred million insects for every human on Earth.

Insects damage our crops, our trees, and our houses. The corn earworm can lay waste to a field of corn. Bark beetles, which are about the size of a grain of rice, can destroy a forest.

Carpenter ants tunnel into the beams in our houses to make their own homes.

So would the world be better off without insects?

At first glance, as you brush away that bothersome fly, you might think that the answer is yes. It would be a world without fleas on the dog and a world without ants crawling over the kitchen counter. It would be a world without mosquitoes that spread malaria. It would be a world without yellow jackets that sting, and a world without worms in your apple.

It would, however, be a world without apples. We wouldn't see colorful butterflies drinking nectar from the flowers. There would be no flowers. Bees, flies, beetles, moths, and butterflies all play an important role in pollination, so there would be no seeds for the next generation of plants.

Insects are also an important part of the food chain. Not only do they thrive by eating one another, they also provide food for animals higher up the food chain. Many kinds of birds, fish, and mammals live on a diet of insects. If it were not for insects, a lot of creatures, including us, would go hungry.

In a world without insects, you'd also miss meeting weird and icky creatures such as the termite queen with a body the size of a potato and the shriveled zombie ant hanging from a leaf above its nest. And you'd miss meeting the beetle that spends its childhood in a ball of dung.

CHAPTER 1

Stranger than Fiction

In the fading light, the dead body lay half-hidden in the grass. Inch by inch, it began to move. It came to rest on a patch of bare, sandy soil. Slowly the body began to sink into the ground. It appeared to be burying itself. By morning, the body was gone.

This sounds like a scene from a horror movie.

But the dead body, which happened to belong to a mouse, had help in its disappearing act. Attracted by the smell of decay, two burying beetles had flown in and tunneled under the body. Lying on their backs, they used their strong legs, to propel the mouse forward. Every now and then, a beetle emerged from the tail end and ran around to the head end. The beetles were acting together like a conveyer belt.

A burying beetle's antennae match the colors on its hard outer wings.

When they reached a place where the ground was right, the beetles turned over and started to dig. They were still hidden under the mouse. Why would beetles go to the bother of burying a dead mouse? The answer is that they were providing food for their young. After they buried the mouse, the female beetle laid around fifteen eggs next to the decaying corpse. Unlike most insects, burying beetles are responsible parents. When the eggs hatch, both parents take on the task of feeding their hungry grubs a diet of puréed mouse. Their job is done when the grubs stop eating and go into their resting stage. The parent beetles then tunnel upward into the daylight to begin their search for another body.[1]

The burying beetle is a big, handsome insect. It is about 1.5 inches (4 cm) long. Like all beetles, it has a hard body with two shell-like outer wings protecting the two thin flying wings. The outer wings are black with bright orange markings, and it has a matching orange tuft on the end of each of its antennae. Beetles are the most numerous kind of insect. Their hard bodies allow them to survive in almost any habitat.

Super Strong

For their size, insects are incredibly strong. If you could jump like a grasshopper, you would be able to clear a football field in one leap. An ant can carry a load four times its own weight in its jaws. That's like you picking up a 300- or 400-pound

Zombie Ant

Leaving the safety of its nest, an ant climbs a nearby stem. At exactly 25 centimeters (about 10 inches) above the forest floor, it clamps its jaws into a leaf and hangs motionless. Its brain has been taken over by the zombie ant fungus. The fungus has told the ant to stop where the micro-climate is perfect for it to grow inside the ant's body. Soon fungal spores rain down on the nest below. Then the grue-some scene is repeated. Another zombie ant leaves the nest to climb a stem and hang help-lessly from a leaf exactly 25 centimeters above the forest floor.

(136- or 181-kilogram) weight with your teeth. An insect's strength comes from having its muscles joined to large areas of its tough exoskeleton.

An insect's exoskeleton is a bit like the armor worn by knights back in the fifteenth century. However, unlike the knight, the insect doesn't sweat or have trouble breathing underneath its armor. The insect is cold blooded. Its body temperature goes up and down with the temperature of its surroundings. It doesn't have a nose or lungs. Instead it has spiracles, or air holes, along the sides of its body that lead to breathing tubes.

Bursting at the Seams

An exoskeleton has a lot of advantages when it comes to strength and safety. However, it has one big disadvantage. It cannot grow. To get bigger, an insect has to molt or shed its hard skeleton. It molts anywhere from three to twenty times during its life, depending on the kind of insect. Underneath the old skin is a new, soft skin that lets the insect's body expand. The new exoskeleton slowly hardens. This is a high-risk time for the insect. While the exoskeleton is still soft, the insect cannot fly or run away from its enemies. Until the new skin is hard, it cannot support much weight. This limits the size to which an insect can grow.

The exoskeleton completely covers the insect. It covers its antennae, or feelers, and lines its breathing tubes. The exoskeleton even covers its eyes.

Insects see a different world than we do. Because each eye has hundreds of lenses, insects don't see details. However, their eyes are great for detecting movement. That's why it's so hard to swat a fly.

Sometimes big changes happen between one molt and the next. A butterfly, for example, starts out as an egg. Then it becomes a caterpillar; then a chrysalis; and finally an adult butterfly. This way of growing is called metamorphosis, which means "change of shape." The change that occurs when a chrysalis turns into an adult is one of the wonders of nature. Inside the chrysalis, the caterpillar cells dissolve into a kind of caterpillar soup. Over the course of two weeks or so, the cells in the soup form into a completely different creature with a slender body and colorful wings. The chewing mouth parts of the caterpillar are replaced by the sucking mouthparts of a butterfly that flutters off to sip nectar from flowers. Some insects, such as grasshoppers, go through

The life cycle of the monarch butterfly is an example of complete metamorphosis. The caterpillar hatches from an egg (*left*), turns into a chrysalis (*top middle*), and finally emerges as a beautiful butterfly.

incomplete metamorphosis. Young grasshoppers look like their parents, but they are smaller and don't have wings.

What's for Dinner?

Insects often behave in weird ways. Female praying mantises have been known to eat their mates. A hungry mother insect sometimes gobbles up her own children. This is usually a case of mistaken identity, however. Those hundred eyes are not good for recognizing faces, and there's an added problem when the kids don't look like their parents.

Insects usually try to make life easy for the next generation by laying their eggs where their offspring will find their favorite food. One kind of small wasp makes sure her little grubs don't go hungry by laying her eggs inside fat caterpillars. When the wasp eggs hatch, the grubs are surrounded by their favorite food—caterpillar guts! A grub is careful not to be too greedy. It likes its food fresh, so it doesn't kill off its host right away. It just nibbles the caterpillar's insides while the caterpillar is nibbling leaves. The caterpillar spins a cocoon, but what finally comes out is not a colorful moth or butterfly. By this time, the caterpillar has been devoured, and a small wasp emerges.

It takes a lot of food to satisfy the trillions of insects that share our world. When an insect lives on our food, such as corn, we call it a "bad" insect. An insect that destroys the grub that eats our food is a "good" insect. Insects that pollinate flowers are also good insects. Without them, we would not have most kinds of fruits and vegetables.

The insects that end up being eaten are an important link in the food chain. They provide a valuable source of protein for many species of birds, mammals, and fish. In Asia, South America, and Africa, several kinds of insects and grubs are included in the

Fried grasshoppers make a tasty meal.

human diet. Grasshoppers become "good" insects when they are served caramelized as a healthy snack.[2] In Nepal, *bakuti*, a paste made from mashed bee pupae, is a big favorite. Bakuti looks rather like scrambled eggs and has a nutty taste.

In Thailand, there are twenty thousand small farms that raise crickets for human food.[3] They provide a source of protein that is much less hard on the environment than raising cattle and poultry. In the Western world, we don't like the thought of eating bugs, though it's not so very different than eating shrimp and crab. To make better use of the world's resources, we should be looking for ways to make insects more appetizing.

CHAPTER 2

Ugly Wins!

Mirror, mirror on the wall, who is the ugliest one of all? As the insects parade in front of the mirror, who is going to win the Ugly Insect Contest? Extra points would surely be given for size. As far as insects go, big is ugly. When an insect is big, you can see all those spines and bristles. You can see its waving antennae and its fluttering wings. You can look into those bulging bug eyes.

Crane flies have long, dangling legs that help them balance while they rest in the waving grass. When a bird attacks a crane fly, sometimes all it gets is a beakful of legs.[1] The legs break off, and the crane fly flutters away, happy to live a little longer. But the legs don't grow back. Adult crane flies look better to us than their children. A young crane fly is a large gray blob of a maggot. It has no legs, and it has so little shape that it is hard to tell its head from its tail end.

A giant walking stick pretends to be a prickly twig.

Wacky Walkers

The Australian walking stick is another big, ugly insect. Like many insects, it is camouflaged so that it blends into its surroundings. That's not easy when you are almost 6 inches (15 cm) long and have a large, plump, spiny body. When a walking stick is scared, it sways gently, trying to look like a dry leaf shaking in the wind. It often curves up its tail end. If its enemies don't think it's a leaf, maybe they'll think that it stings like a scorpion. The fierce look is all a bluff, though. Walking sticks don't sting or bite.

The female walking stick is too fat to fly; her wings are small flaps. The male is much skinnier than the female, and he has wings that allow him to fly. He uses them to cruise around in search of a mate.

Battling Beetles

The rhinoceros beetle is one of the largest insects on earth. The female uses her large snout to burrow into wood. She gives off a scent that attracts the male beetles. If two males show up at the same time, they wrestle with their strong mouthparts, and they fight to the death. In Thailand, beetle fighting is a national sport. People stage fights and bet on the winner.

The Goliath beetle is another insect giant with a long snout. It lives in Africa and only eats fruit.

Her tiny subjects surround the giant termite queen.

Compared with its giant cousins, the bombardier beetle is quite small, but it does have a weird and ugly way of protecting itself. It uses chemical warfare. When a bombardier beetle senses danger, it lowers its tail end between its legs and shoots out a cloud of poison gas, which can kill other insects. The gas can also burn skin and leaves a brown stain. If you're close enough, you can actually hear a little pop. Most bombardiers get off no more than four or five shots before recharging, but Thomas Eisner at Cornell University once met up with a twenty-nine-shooter.[2]

The Potato Queen

One of the prizes in the Ugly Insect Contest would surely go to the termite queen, which lives in Africa. An ugly thing about insects is the way they move. They scuttle or dart or flutter. However, this termite queen doesn't move at all. Her legs are far too small to support the weight of her huge pale body, which is the size of a potato.

Termites are social insects; several kinds live together in a nest—soldiers, workers, kings, and queens. The queen is really just an egg-laying machine, She can lay as many as eight thousand eggs in a single day. Some termite queens live for fifty years.

Beautiful but Scary

One insect that wouldn't get many points in the Ugly Insect Contest is the butterfly. The butterfly's beauty is a kind of protection. Birds are warned off by its bold, bright colors. To a bird, the eyespots on the wings of a peacock butterfly look like owl eyes. The

The Gnarly Dragonfly Nymph

The dragonfly wouldn't win an ugly insect contest either, but its offspring might. Unlike its dazzling, acrobatic parent, a young dragonfly, known as a nymph, has a drab, squat body. It is found in muddy ponds. One of its ugly features is the huge lower lip folded beneath its face. It's like an arm ending in claws. When the nymph spots its prey, the arm-like lip zaps out and grabs it. Then the lip folds back, pulling its struggling victim into its mouth, where the nymph's strong jaws crush it to death.

A puss moth caterpillar can look scary with its weird red head and forked tail.

orange and black of the monarch butterfly's wings are warning colors. Birds have found out that monarchs taste awful. They are also toxic. Viceroy butterflies look like monarchs, and they taste bad, too, but they are not toxic. Birds usually don't eat viceroy butterflies, either.

Some caterpillars use bright colors as protection. When the puss moth caterpillar is scared, it rears up its head end to show a vivid red patch and false eyes. It has a whiplike tail and looks more like a monster than a tasty caterpillar.

CHAPTER 3

Dirty and Deadly Flies

Back in the eighteenth century, Carl Linnaeus (1707–1778) came up with a system for naming plants and animals that is still used to this day. It is called the binomial system of nomenclature.[1] Each plant or animal is given two Latin names: the genus and the species. Our species is *Homo sapiens,* meaning "wise person." The science of naming things is called taxonomy. The person who does it is a taxonomist.

Naming insects is especially difficult because there are so many. It's also difficult because the adults usually don't look like their offspring and grubs that belong to different species may look just like one another. Previously taxonomists had to go through the lengthy process of rearing a grub to find out what adult it belonged to. Sorting this out became easier with advances in genetics. Taxonomists can now use an insect's DNA to separate species.

Insects are also classified into bigger groups called families and even bigger groups called orders. All the members of an order have something in common that separates them from insects in other orders. Flies, for example, belong to the order *Diptera*. True flies have only two wings—a single pair. (Except for those insects that don't have any wings, all others have four wings.) The name *Diptera* comes from the Greek words for "two" and "wing."

The human botfly larva has backward-facing spines on its body. A person can feel this nasty critter wriggling around underneath their skin.

Botflies and Blowflies

Flies have a weird habit of laying their eggs in places where no self-respecting creature would want its kids to grow up: manure piles, dead meat, and living meat.

The horse botfly spends its young stages inside—you guessed it—a horse. The female lays her eggs among the hairs on a horse's front legs. The eggs stay there for weeks, or even months, until the horse licks itself. The moment it does, the eggs hatch. The tiny maggots quickly burrow into the tongue, living inside it for a month. Then they pop out and are swallowed. They spend the next nine months in the horse's gut.

The human botfly doesn't get on people the same way because people don't lick themselves clean. The female hangs around a marsh and lays her eggs on a mosquito. When the mosquito lands on a person, the warmth of the body is a signal for the botfly eggs to hatch. The little creatures burrow into the skin or they may take the easy way in through the mosquito bite.

Eye Worms

In 2016, when a young woman pulled a worm out of her eye, no one believed her until a doctor saw one wiggling across her eyeball. The worms were parasites that spend most of their life cycle in a face fly. They had crawled out of the fly's mouth into the woman's eye when the fly was drinking her tears. Eye worms are found in the eyes of horses or cattle. They are so rare in humans that you don't need to worry about them turning up in your eye! And the young woman was fine after she had pulled fourteen more worms out of her eye.

Another nasty insect is the blowfly, which lays its eggs in open wounds. The maggots live on pus. Even though having blowfly maggots in a wound sounds disgusting, they actually help it heal quicker. During World War I, blowfly maggots were used to clean soldiers' wounds. This treatment is called maggot debridement therapy (MDT). New medicines and surgical techniques replaced this type of treatment after World War II. However, it has been used more and more in recent years. More than two thousand health care centers in the United States have used maggots on wounds, and there is even a brand-name strain called Medical Maggots.[2]

The Unwanted House Guest

Botflies and blowflies cause a lot of problems, but there is another kind of fly that is much more dangerous. It's an insect that everyone knows but few of us fear. It doesn't bite or sting. It is the common housefly. Houseflies can carry millions of bacteria, spreading terrible diseases such as cholera, typhoid, polio, and leprosy.

Houseflies are middle-sized flies. Tiny fruit flies and huge buzzing bluebottles also show up in houses. Fruit flies, house flies, and bluebottles are all different kinds of adult flies. Like other insects, flies go through metamorphosis. There are four stages: egg, maggot, pupa, and adult.

The female housefly lays her eggs in a pile of manure, which is warm and rich in nutrients. The eggs hatch into little white

Houseflies don't bite, but they can be deadly by spreading diseases.

maggots, which grow quickly. In a week, they are eight hundred times heavier than when they hatched. The maggot turns into a pupa, its resting stage. In about a week, it becomes an adult housefly. An adult housefly can live for as long as two months. That's quite a long time for an insect.

Houseflies don't have biting mouth parts. Because they cannot chew, everything they eat must be liquid. When a fly lands on your peanut butter sandwich, the first thing it does is spit on it. Fly spit is so strong that it turns solids to liquids, so the fly can drink some sandwich. A little spit is left behind. The spit contains some of the fly's last meal, which could have been a dead rat or dog droppings. Flies are not picky eaters. They'll eat anything from a cow pie to apple pie.

In spite of all the bad press flies get, there are some species that deserve our gratitude. Without flies to pollinate the cacao tree, we wouldn't have chocolate.

Disease Carriers

Malaria is another disease that was a big killer until people knew how it was spread. Like houseflies, mosquitoes live long enough to lay several batches of eggs. Before a female lays a batch of eggs, she needs a meal of blood, which she gets by tapping into someone's vein. If she bites a person who is sick with malaria, she sucks in malaria parasites along with the blood. She passes these

This mosquito is caught in the act of getting its meal of blood.

parasites to the next person she bites. Only the female mosquito is dangerous; the male doesn't need a blood meal.

Mosquitoes can spread another disease that was first found in Uganda in Africa. In recent years, it has turned up in South America and the southern states of North America. The disease is caused by the Zika virus. When a mosquito that carries this virus bites someone, they may develop flu-like symptoms. The illness can be so mild that the person hardly notices it. But if the mosquito passes the Zika virus on to a pregnant woman, it can cause birth defects in the growing baby. At present there is no cure except to avoid being bitten and by attacking mosquitoes with chemical sprays. It is important to go after the mosquitoes before they have the chance to grow up. The larvae are found in standing water, even in as little water as you might find in an abandoned tire or an old bucket.

CHAPTER 4

Group Homes

Insects mostly look out for themselves. There are, however, some species that live in a community with individuals doing different tasks. They cannot survive alone for long. They are called social insects. The best-known and best-liked of the social insects is the honeybee. Not only do they produce honey and wax, they also pollinate our crops.

People have been keeping bees for thousands of years, but the modern beehive wasn't invented until the mid-nineteenth century.[1] By using bee boxes with movable frames, the beekeeper can collect the honey without destroying the wax comb. Modern beehives can also be moved from place to place. This has led to a whole new industry. Beekeepers are able to load their hives onto trucks and travel northward with the spring, pollinating farm crops as they came into flower. Commercial beekeepers now earn money by providing pollination services as well as by selling

Honeybees are our friends. As well as producing honey, they pollinate our crops.

honey. Backyard bees still pollinate their neighbor's flowers and fruits for free. Without the help of the honeybee, we wouldn't be able to feed the growing world population.

Killer Bees

Killer bees are also social insects, even though, from our point of view, their behavior is antisocial. Even their name sounds deadly. One killer bee is nothing to worry about. Its sting is no worse than the sting of a honeybee. A few thousand stings are a different matter, and that's where the problem lies. Killer bees attack in huge gangs.

Killer bees look a lot like normal honeybees. Even an entomologist has a hard time telling a dead killer bee from a dead honeybee. Killer bees tend to be a little smaller, and they also have slightly shorter tongues. Because bees from the same nest or hive vary in size, you need to measure the bodies and tongues of a lot of bees to be sure you've got killer bees.

With live bees, however, it is a different story. You can tell them apart by the way they act. Killer bees are workaholics. They get up early and go to bed late. Sometimes they even work by moonlight. Killer bee queens lay more eggs and lay them faster than honeybee queens do. Killer bees defend their territory more fiercely. That's how they got the name "killer." They gang up on anything that disturbs their nest. They don't care if its people, pets, or wild animals.

Entomologists call killer bees African or Africanized bees.[2] In the middle of the last century, a scientist brought some African

Vanishing Bees

One day the hive was buzzing with activity. The next day everything was quiet. When the beekeeper checked the hive, she discovered that her bees were gone. All thirty thousand of them! Bees swarm when the hive becomes overcrowded, but this was different. And she knew what was going on. The hive was suffering from a condition that was becoming more and more common. It is called colony collapse disorder (CCD). Nobody knows the cause of the vanishing bees. One suspect is a family of pesticides with a long name—neonicotinoids. Scientists are struggling to find an answer and a cure.

queen bees to Brazil. He wanted to breed them with honeybees from Europe. He hoped to produce hardworking bees that would do well in Brazil's hot climate. While he was doing his experiments, some swarms escaped. Because killer bees are restless and hardworking, they spread quickly. The males mated with a local beekeeper's queens.

The new bees swarmed to the north and to the south. They invaded other countries. Killer bees have reached the southern United States. Cool winters should stop their northward spread. They sound terrifying, but it is very unlikely you'll ever be attacked by killer bees. If you are, don't try to fight them off. The best thing you can do is to run for your life. It's better to dive through bushes and trees than to stay in the open.

The people with the most to lose are those who depend on bees for their living. If killer bees take over a hive, this means trouble for beekeepers because killer bees are hard to work with. It's not just that they sting; they also swarm and fly off. Killer bees like to be on the move.

March of the Ants

There are many different kinds of ants, and most of them are strange. Some keep slaves; they raid other colonies and bring prisoners home to do the work. Some tend their own underground gardens; they grow fungus to eat and bring in leaves to

Army ants are blind, but they have huge, powerful jaws that tear up any victims they discover by smell.

nurture their fungal gardens. Some store honey in the bodies of members of their group, turning them into live honey pots. But strangest of all are the army ants. Like killer bees, these fierce ants always like to be on the move.

With their quarter-inch (0.6-cm) jaws that tear at flesh, army ants leave behind a grim trail of death wherever they go. Small skeletons cover the ground of villages they march through. The ants take care of the rats and mice. But one of the strangest things about army ants is that they have no eyes. They find their victims by smell. Millions of them form a column a few feet wide, smelling out anything that is alive. The queen and grubs are carried along by the workers. Nothing stops the column—not even running water. When they come to a stream, they lock their legs together, and the front ants drift out into the water. When they touch the other bank, they hang on, forming a living bridge across the water. The rest of the ants cross the stream on the backs of their comrades.

After a few weeks of raiding, the ants settle down for a spell of domestic life. They form a huge ball. It is just like a regular ants' nest, except that the walls are made of ants' bodies. There are tunnels and little rooms. The queen lives near the middle. She begins to lay eggs, and other ants tend to the larvae when they hatch. Soon the pupae from the last egg-laying become adults. Then the army gets ready for another raid.

Hungry Locusts

Another rampaging insect is the locust. Locusts have stripped fields bare ever since people first started planting crops. Although they travel in gangs, locusts are not social insects. They have no queen, and they have no home. For a long time, no one knew what happened to them in years when they didn't swarm; they vanished.

The mystery was solved by Boris Uvarov (1889–1970) in 1921.[3] He found out that locusts lead a double life. Some years they are loners; other years they go around in gangs. When they join a

A locust rests on a fence. Lone locusts are as harmless as regular grasshoppers. It's when they swarm that causes trouble.

gang, they take on a new look. They don't act as they did when they were on their own. They wear their gang colors, and they become greedier and wilder.

As loners, they look and act like other grasshoppers. Their green and tan colors blend into the background. They nibble on grass. They can live in this harmless way for generations. Then, when the weather and grass are right, more eggs are laid and those eggs all hatch. Young hoppers fight with other young hoppers for food, reacting to overcrowding. They all begin to eat more. Their color changes; instead of blending in with the grass, they are now red, yellow, and black. Their legs grow longer. Huge swarms of excited little hoppers cover the ground.

When the hoppers are full grown, they have wings and take to the air, flying downwind. The real journey has begun. By now, there are so many that they darken the sky. They are very much like an invading army. Wherever they land, they strip the plants and trees bare, leaving a wide path of destruction.

Locusts fly wherever the wind takes them. Scientists from many countries banded together to fight them. They drew up battle plans; they used planes and chemicals. Then they realized that the best way to stop locusts is to not let them get started. Scientists now keep track of rainfall records all over the world. When the weather is right for locusts, they send out locust alerts. The aim is to keep those little hoppers from joining gangs in the first place.

CHAPTER 5

Recycling Agents

At first glance, a beetle scurrying across the ground doesn't look as if it was designed to fly. This is especially true if the beetle is a scarab beetle, pushing along a ball of dirt. The ball is often bigger than the beetle. But, like all beetles, the scarab has wings—two pairs. The front two wings form a hard case protecting the thin, flying wings.

The ancient Egyptians greatly admired scarab beetles The scarab pushing its ball made them think of the great god Ra rolling the sun across the sky. They often made beetle jewelry with gems for the wings. They used pure gold for the ball. In real life, scarab beetles make their balls out of dung. In Egypt, they mostly use camel dung. In other places, they use horse or cow dung. In Africa, elephant dung is popular. Some of the scarab beetles in Africa are huge. Big beetles need a big supply of dung.

It's no wonder the Egyptians admired the handsome scarab beetle. This little critter's exoskeleton shines like copper.

But why do scarabs roll balls of dung all over the place? They do this because they are looking for somewhere to bury the dung ball so young scarabs can eat them.

Scarab larvae are raised on dung. They like their dung fresh. The adults bury the dung so that it doesn't dry out. This is important in places such as Egypt where the climate is hot and dry. Beetles rolling balls of dung around are looking for soft ground. When they find a place that suits them, they start to dig. When the hole is deep enough, they push the ball down into it. The female lays her eggs in the dung ball. Then the hole is filled in. After the eggs hatch, the larvae feast on the dung. When the larvae grow into adults, they crawl out of the ground.

Scarabs find dung by its smell. Several beetles often work on the same cowpat. A scarab has a rake on its head that it uses to scoop up dung. While it works, it sorts out the fiber, only keeping the juiciest stuff. It shapes the ball against its body with its middle and back pairs of legs. While rolling the ball away, the scarab hangs on to it with its two front legs. Meanwhile, it rotates the ball with its other four legs, so the ball ends up perfectly smooth and round.

Beetle Watching

A French naturalist named Jean-Henri Fabre (1823–1915) spent hours and hours watching dung beetles.[1] He noticed that some beetles prefer a life of crime to one of hard work. One beetle was happily rolling away his ball. Another zoomed down and landed on top of the ball, hoping to scare away the rightful owner. The first beetle set the ball rolling, trying to get the would-be thief to fall off the dung ball. When this didn't work, the beetles joined forces and rolled the ball away together. The second beetle still had a backup plan. While the first beetle was digging a hole to bury the dung ball, he made off with it. Fabre wondered if the beetles really were that smart. He thought up some experiments to test

This beetle is rolling a ball of dung bigger than itself.

their intelligence. Sometimes a small twig spears the ball, and the beetles have to work it loose. So Fabre decided to nail a dung ball to the ground with a straight pin. The beetle team that had been pushing the ball was puzzled when it wouldn't move. They walked around it for a while, and then one burrowed under it like someone looking under the hood of a stalled car. Finally, the beetle spotted the pin. It seemed to realize that the pin was causing the problem. Both beetles got under the ball and used their strong backs to lift it up. They raised the ball higher and higher. Soon, they were standing on the very tips of their claws. With one last heave, they pushed the ball off the top of the pin.

Next, Fabre stuck a longer pin through the ball. Would one of the beetles think of climbing onto the other's back so that they could lift the ball even higher? The beetles weren't that smart! In fact, insects aren't very smart at all. They operate by instinct. They can only solve problems if the answer is in their genes.

Bigger Is Better

Bernd Heinrich (1940–) spent a lot of time in Africa watching beetles give elephant dung a working over.[2] *Heliocopris*, the biggest elephant dung beetle, doesn't roll dung away. It makes a hole right under the dung pile. It has strong digging blades on the front of its head and on the side of its front legs. It's built rather like a flying backhoe. The male and female beetles dig the hole together.

When it's deep enough, the male tosses down bundles of dung to the female, who shapes them into balls. She then lays an egg in each ball. The male then seals up the hole. The female stays down there. The hole becomes her tomb.

About two thousand different species of beetles in Africa live in dung. Some of them eat the dung right where it is. Others make dung balls and roll them away. A one-inch-long (2.5 cm) beetle can make dung balls the size of a baseball. When Bernd Heinrich set up beetle races on smooth ground, he found that the fastest ones rolled at a speed of 8 inches (20 cm) per second.

Yellow Jacket Cleanup Crew

Beetles have the help of other insects in keeping the world clean. Yellow jackets thrive on a high-protein diet. That's why you find them hovering over your barbequed chicken at a picnic. They snatch a mouthful of meat and carry it back to the nest. Soon other yellow jackets are buzzing around. Yellow jackets actually prefer their meat raw. When some unlucky songbird meets a tragic end, the yellow jackets gather. They start tearing at its flesh until there's nothing left but feathers and bones. The yellow jackets have done their job as part of nature's recycling crew.

Scarabs Down Under

Scarab beetles clean up a lot of dung. People found out how important they are when cattle were introduced into Australia. A cow puts out twelve dung pats a day, each weighing about 3.75 pounds (1.70 kg). Australia's thirty million cows were producing 67,200 tons (61,000 metric tonnes) of manure each day. Australia is a big country, but with that many cows and no beetles, it was in danger of being buried in manure. So beetles were brought in from Africa. The cleanup crew went to work and solved the problem.

It's not quite true to say that there were no dung beetles in Australia when cattle were first brought in; the kangaroo dung beetle was already there. This beetle doesn't like cow dung, which is just as well for the cows. It doesn't make dung balls as others do. It doesn't even wait for the dung to drop. It lays its eggs in a kangaroo's rectum; that way the young get their dung fresh. This also qualifies the kangaroo dung beetle for the prize for the strangest lifestyle in the insect world.

Chapter Notes

Chapter 1. Stranger than Fiction

1. Hannah Nordhaus, "Beetle Resurrection," *Scientific American,* December 2017, p. 67.
2. Arnold van Huis, Henk van Gurp, and Marcel Dicke, *The Insect Cookbook: Food for a Sustainable Planet* (New York, NY: Columbia University Press, 2014), p. 41.
3. Arnold van Huis, Henk van Gurp, and Marcel Dicke, *The Insect Cookbook: Food for a Sustainable Planet*, p. 8

Chapter 2. Ugly Wins!

1. Erica McAlister, "Making the Case for Flies," *Natural History,* February 2018, p. 28.
2. Loris J. Milne and Marjorie Milne, *Insect Worlds* (New York, NY: Charles Scribner's Sons, 1980), p. 9.

Chapter 3. Dirty and Deadly Flies

1. Margaret J. Anderson, *Carl Linnaeus: Father of Classification* (Berkeley Heights, NJ: Enslow Publishers, Inc., 1997), p. 12.
2. "Frequently Asked Questions," Monarch Labs, 2017, http://www.monarchlabs.com/faq.

Chapter 4. Group Homes

1. Fergus Chadwick, Steve Alton, Emma Sarah Tennant, Bill Fitzmaurice, and Judy Earl, *The Bee Book* (New York, NY: DK Publishing, 2016), p. 33.
2. Laurence Pringle, *Killer Bees* (New York, NY: Morrow Junior Books, 1990), p. 33.
3. L. H. Newman, *Man and Insects* (New York, NY: Natural History Press, 1966), p. 132.

Chapter 5. Recycling Agents

1. Margaret J. Anderson, *Children of Summer: Henri Fabre's Insects* (New York, NY: Farrar, Straus and Giroux, 1997), pp. 67–71.
2. Bernd Heinrich, *In a Patch of Fireweed* (Cambridge, MA: Harvard University Press, 1984), pp. 101–109.

Glossary

antennae (singular, antenna) Feelers on the head of an insect.

arthropod An animal with jointed limbs, a segmented body, and its skeleton on the outside.

entomologist A scientist who studies insects.

exoskeleton An external skeleton.

insect An animal with three body parts, six legs, and an exoskeleton.

larva (plural, larvae) The stage of an insect between the egg and the pupa. Caterpillars, maggots, and grubs are all larvae.

maggot Young stages of a fly; the word is usually used to describe a larva without legs.

metamorphosis Changes in form and shape that take place between the time an insect hatches and its mature adult stage.

microclimate The growing conditions in a very small area.

nymph A young insect that does not go through complete metamorphosis.

pesticide A chemical used to destroy insects or other things harmful to plants.

pollination The transfer of pollen from the male parts of a plant to the female parts of the plant, often done by insects.

pupa (plural pupae) The stage between the larva and the adult. During this stage the insect goes through a complete metamorphosis.

spiracle One of several small holes along the body through which an insect breathes.

spore The equivalent of a seed for a fungus.

taxonomy The study of classification.

Further Reading

Books

Buckley, James, Jr. *Bugs!* New York, NY: Liberty Street, 2017.

Chadwick, Fergus, Steve Alton, Emma Sarah Tennant, Bill Fitzmaurice, and Judy Earl. *The Bee Book*. London, UK: DK Publishing, 2016.

Honovich, Nancy. *1,000 Facts About Insects.* Washington, DC: National Geographic Children's Books, 2018.

Zborowski, Paul. *World's Weirdest Bugs: The Tiny Aliens Among Us*. London, UK: New Holland Publishers, 2018.

Websites

Amateur Entomologists' Society
www.amentsoc.org/insects/fact-files/a-to-z-of-insects.html
Dive deeper by looking up specific insects using this A-to-Z list.

Museum Victoria Australia
museumsvictoria.com.au/bugs/index.aspx
Learn more about bugs and their lives and why they are important.

National Geographic Kids
kids.nationalgeographic.com/animals/hubs/insects
Watch videos and read facts about ants, termites, butterflies, beetles, and more.

Index